# THE PEOPLE OF THE RIVER

NORTHWATER

**CONSTANTINE ISSIGHOS**

Copyright 2012 © Constantine Issighos. Published in Canada. Printed in U.S.A. No part of this book may be reproduced or transmitted in any form or by any means, electronic or mechanical, including photocopying, recording, and/or by any information storage and retrieval system except by a reviewer who may quote brief passages in a review to be printed in a magazine, newspaper, or on the web without written permission in writing from the author/publisher. For information, please contact www.awaqkunabooks.com

NorthWater is an imprint of Awaqkuna Books Inc.

**Vol. 2 of THE AMAZON EXPLORATION SERIES:**
*THE PEOPLE OF THE RIVER*

Library and Archives Canada

ISBN 978-0-9878599-1-4

Library and Archives Canada Cataloguing in Publication

ATTENTION CHILDRENS ASSOCIATIONS, BOOK STORES, PUBLIC OR PRIVATE LIBRARIES: quantity discounts are available on bulk purchases of this book series.

# THE AMAZON EXPLORATION SERIES

Children's Books

by

Constantine Issighos

| | |
|---|---|
| 1 | Upper Amazon Voyage by River Boat |
| 2 | The People of the River |
| 3 | The Children of the River |
| 4 | Amazon's Nature of Things |
| 5 | Echoes of Nature: a Beautiful Wild Habitat |
| 6 | The Amazon Rainforest |
| 7 | Amazonian Sisterhood |
| 8 | Amazon River Wolves |
| 9 | Amazonian Landscapes and Sunsets |
| 10 | Amazonian Canopy: the Roof of the World's Rainforest |
| 11 | Amazonian Tribes: a World of Difference |
| 12 | Birds and Butterflies of the Amazon |
| 13 | The Great Wonders of the Amazon |
| 14 | The Jaguar People |
| 15 | The Fresh Water Giants |
| 16 | The Call of the Shaman |
| 17 | Indigenous Families: Life in Harmony with Nature |
| 18 | Amazon in Peril |
| 19 | Giant Tarantulas and Centipedes |

The Amazon rainforest has had five thousand years of human settlement. Long before the 16th century, before the arrival of the Europeans, sizable and sedentary complex societies existed in the Amazon rainforest. These indigenous societies cleared sections of the rainforest for agriculture and managed the forests to optimize the ecological realities of their environment. Through their close association with their *terra firma,* they saw the importance to their survival of maintaining a productive biodiversity. Through a combination of open fields and natural forest, they left areas to be dominated by species of special interest to humans.

Out of necessity, a large number of indigenous settlements were established along the complex Amazonian river system and its tributaries. The inhabitants developed a good means of transportation; they fished and used the fertile floodlands for agriculture.

While in Loreto, Peru, I was one of the visitors who journeyed into the Upper Amazon River, travelling the Maranon and Ucayali rivers from *Yurimaguas* to Iquitos. Standing by the Maranon riverbanks, I looked at life so lush, so green and so alive. Nutrient-rich soil washed from the steep mountains creates here a higher biodiversity than is found anywhere else in the world. The Amazon River and its hundreds of tributaries flow slowly across the landscape with an extremely shallow gradient as it heads towards the sea. I photographed people and indigenous communities who live side-by-side with others who came to settle here from different parts of the world. I photographed and interviewed the *people of the river* who are desperately trying to hang onto their traditional ways while adjusting to the demands of the outsiders, the cattle ranchers, coffee farmers, loggers, miners, oil workers and government agents. The lives of the indigenous people are on a fast track forward, so it was a relief for me to capture the timeless aspects of their daily lives--fishing, cooking, collecting medicinal plants, participating in ceremonies, hunting and river bathing. These photographs clearly remind me of what the people of the river ask: no money or luxuries, just the freedom of choice to live as they wish.

Many times, I have been drawn back to my photos of the people of the river. Photographing them in their natural state offered the opportunity to experience their spirit of integrity, ingenuity, purity and their lifestyle in harmony with the rainforest. They live in an amazing ecosystem with an incredible variety of exotic birds, giant buttressed trees, colourful bromeliads, as well as jaguars, tapirs and other jungle animals. Pink dolphins, at play in the rivers, are accompanied by other fresh water giants such as arapaima, giant otters and manatees.

The Amazon River, along with its tributaries' drainage, is home to giant freshwater fish species. The world's aquariums have found some of the most beautiful, interesting and exotic specimens here. This extraordinary aquatic biodiversity evolved from an ancient line of species that were already established over 130 million years ago and they have changed little since that time. The most commonly accepted biological theory regarding these species is that their precursors evolved during a geological period when what is now South America, Africa, southern Asia and Australia formed a single continent called *Gondwanaland*. Upon the separation of these continents, these fish ancestors then evolved independently. Today, their modern descendents in the Amazon have speciated into thousands of endemic varieties.

Imagine yourself as one of the people of the river, drifting down a winding waterway surrounded on both sides by a lush, endless sea of tropical greenery, and all that separates you from the deep gray Amazon waters is a long narrow handmade canoe. As you manoeuvre around flowing logs, something unidentified crashes off into the underbrush and you catch a glimpse of a magnificent fish startled into a dive.

Suddenly, the rainforest above the riverbank greenery erupts with a roar so loud that all you can imagine is some giant fierce predator on the prowl. But as you turn to face your destiny, the imagined menace is revealed to be a group of furry red howler monkeys huddled together in the tree canopy. With a sigh of relief you continue onward, deeper into your intended destination. This is one of the many sensations I experienced as I neared Monkey Island, a haven for nature lovers who fully desire to experience the wonders of the tropical rainforest.

The Upper Amazon doesn't have shopping malls with air-conditioning or gourmet restaurants, but the world's biggest forest offers unique and spectacular features. No one can be indifferent to the croaks of the frogs and toads at night, to the chant of the monkeys in the forest before evening rainstorms, or to the brutal power of these storms and the way they interact with the inhabitants of the forest. No one can be indifferent to the unbelievably immense green, the large expanse of water and to the web of life in evidence everywhere. It is part of our ancestral roots as human beings, that here, in the tropics, in places such as the Upper Amazon River, lies our unwritten history. Traveling upstream, I always feel an intense sense of smallness, of wonder, and yet a calm familiarity.

The Amazon River affects the rainforest and its inhabitants because both need the river for their survival. Native people's diet consists of fruit, including bananas, avocados, mangos, and sweet palm; Brazil nuts; insects; potatoes and cassava. The Amazon River and its countless tributaries also function as the chief means of transportation for the indigenous communities to trade and exchange green produce, meat and fish.

The river also serves as a social communication route, as villagers sometimes invite other villagers to ceremonies and feasts. Invited guests travel in long canoes for many miles for these events, thus building strong ties among villagers of different tribes. In these feasts, the menu might include plantain soup, smoked monkey, wild turkey, piranha and arapaima fish. As a gift for accepting an invitation, the host village may give out ceramic pots, machetes or cooked food. The visitors reciprocate the host by inviting them to a feast in their village.

Walking along the well-marked river banks is as if you were walking through another world. The jungle on one side is a wall of multi-shaded green from the ground to the canopy, with moss covering the trunks, and plant upon plant hanging from every bit of bark. Creepers and vines wind their way around the giant trees, and bright red flowers suspend themselves on flimsy stalks in mid-air. Tiny streams trickle through mossy rocks and prehistoric vegetation that looks like mini-palms sprouting beside the riverbank, the shade of their leaves ruffled by a slight breeze.

Bird nests are hidden in the brushes next to the paths. If you look closely you can hear squeaking coming from within the bushes. Brown-winged birds with red or yellow bellies fly past you every few minutes. If you are lucky, you can look up and spy a parrot on a banch above you, its long green feathers curving down, adding to the magical setting. Other birds hoot from the tree tops, but they are difficult to spot through the thick greenery. It is a most beautiful corner of the world, with trails that climb gently through perfect, untouched greenery. As the trails climb, the view of the narrow rows of cultivated plots of banana plants opens out below you. The land slopes downward again towards indigenous settlements surrounded by undisturbed hills.

As far as the eye can see, the surface of the Amazon river is covered in thick deep green, undisturbed by boat traffic. It is then that you realize the legacy of the Amazon river and the forest that surrounds you. The marked paths are easy to follow, some leading to settlements while others lead further into the jungle. You need to be careful if you choose to go down the paths that are muddy, slippery and steep. The frequent rainstorms cause mudslides here making the paths wider and obliterating some of the vegetation. Sit still for a while and enjoy the tranquility that surrounds you.

As I travel through the provincial jungle of Loreto, Peru, I recall the words of the naturalist Gerald Durrell, *"There is nothing like a tropical rainforest for replacing arrogance with awe."* It humbles me to be in one of the Earth's last frontiers. The Upper Amazon rainforest is a primordial place, dark and mysterious even in daytime. Vibrant and alive with rarely seen flora and fauna, it is one of the most complex, beautiful and important ecosystems on this Earth. As the name rainforest suggests, the sun is strong and the environment is warm, moist and stable. Without exaggerating, when it comes to inspiring wonder, the Upper Amazon rainforest has no rival.

Covering almost a third of Peruvian territory, densely vegetated and criss-crossed by tributaries—most of them navigable—its jungle is little visited and sparsely populated. Indigenous people—uncontacted tribes—still inhabit some of its forest.

Deep in the Upper Amazon jungle, just south of Maranon River, lays a largely unexplored area of 5 million acres practically untouched by humans. The only humans present are a handful of rangers living in primitive conditions in a few scattered leaf huts. There are no indigenous villagers or temporary residents nor are there tourist facilities. Nearby is the area known as *Lagunas*, called the Pacaya-Samiria "la selva de los espejos"--the jungle of mirrors. This land is the largest national reserve—land protected by the central government—in Peru. To enter the reserve, one needs a permit which is issued only for scientific or exploratory purposes. Only 40% of the Pacaya-Samiria reserve has been explored. Botanists, naturalists and investigators of medicinal plants are given brief entry periods to conduct their research.

Indigenous tribes in the Upper Amazon basin inhabit varied environments; some live in the grassland, some in the beautiful tropical rainforest and others in the scrub. Because of this, the means of survival is also extremely varied. Some groups only have 30 or fewer members. Indigenous groups have had different experiences with outsiders—not necessarily tourists. Typically indigenous groups live by fishing, hunting and growing and gathering of plants to be used for food, shelter and medicinal purposes. The "Jaguar people" have a powerful instinct for survival when hunting for prey—an instinct shared by other non-human night predators in the jungle. I had little difficulty finding an appropriated name for them--the *"Jaguar People."*

Although they hunt for various animals in the rainforest, monkeys are the primary source of food. The Brazilian tribe of Matis is known for their fishing and hunting skills. They are also known for wearing facial ornaments believed to be a mystical homage to the jaguar and its incredible hunting skills. In fact, these hunters use blow guns that are accurate up to 30 meters (100 feet). However, since there has been little contact with this tribe, there is not much known about their lives. It's been recorded that the group consists of about 130 members. In recent years there has been a slight increase.

The long canoe sliced through the river water, sending out a narrow wake on the otherwise perfectly smooth mirror-like grey surface. It was not yet the turn of the seasons; soon however, the floodwaters would rise. For the time being, the trees were still only knee-deep in water. My guide Willy and I continued paddling through the dark, mysterious forest tributary scouting for anything interesting to photograph.

It was soon time to return to civilization. Tomorrow we would rise with the sun and hopefully catch a ride with the first available river barge. It would sail slowly during the next few days, and the swamps and wetlands would be left behind.

The primary purpose of my trip was to photograph wildlife in its natural surroundings. Once away from human habitat, one has to be patient to see wildlife in the remote jungle. I came away with a healthy respect for the survival skills that an indigenous person needs to live in the Upper Amazon. A visitor certainly needs protection against insects, reptiles and nocturnal predatory animals. I did not feel that the rainforest is inherently dangerous for the indigenous inhabitants who have much knowledge about jungle survival. They know how to use the sap from certain trees against intestinal discomfort, insect bites and as an insect repellent. They know how to grow their own food, how to hunt and fish and how to use their poisonous darts to kill their prey. They know that the *Rio Amazonas* is their lifeline, their means of transportation and communication with the world beyond. They are excellent canoe-makers and navigators; their rituals still organize time and space in their villages. Above all, they know that they are the sole protectors of the environment that provides them with the means of survival and the perpetuation of their indigenous lifestyle.

*The Amazon Exploration Series*            *Constantine Issighos*

*The People of the River*

*In seasonal flood areas, people build their homes on 30 ft. high posts. The wooden walkways serve as docking facilities for row-boats.*

*Off season, the same fields serve as a children's playground, an adult's sports field, a shortcut path or as a vegetable and flower garden. Also, since there are no indoor toilets, out-houses are used*

*The "People of the River" are feeling the pressure of "civilization" advancing on their territories. Oil companies, gold mining, logging and giant agro-business have introduced a "money economy" that goes against their traditional values.*

*Many natives are now living in cities. They crave consumer goods, and have exchanged their traditional palm-thatched houses for zinc roofs, their hunting spears for rifles and their active forest life for viewing TV sitcoms. In such city dwellings (pueblo joven) garbage is everywhere, waiting to be swept away by the river's next flooding season.*

Roofs are made of palm tree leaves that appear to be strong enough to protect people from powerful rain storms. Every year before the rain season, the roofs need to be replaced with new palm tree leaves.

*Standing at the outskirts of the Amazonian city of Iquitos, I realized the negative effects of peoples' uprooting, their severe poverty and sense of hopelessness.*

*People of the River maintain their ancestral tradition of living off the rainforest by cultivating floodplain soils for farming, by fishing and by being part of a healthy communal lifestyle.*

*The river system is their lifeline. They have adapted their comm.-unity structure to their environment which allows them to have a sustainable living.*

*The river system is thus their main transportation route to travel and trade, socialize with other tribes and maintain their community.*

*The river is also the children's playground, where they spend considerable time refreshing and enjoying themselves.*

*The Amazon Exploration Series*                                          *Constantine Issighos*

*The People of the River*

*A typical fruit market buzzing with activity.*

*Fish, river-turtles and worms are cooked in river-side eateries.*

www.ingramcontent.com/pod-product-compliance
Lightning Source LLC
Chambersburg PA
CBHW041755040426
42446CB00001B/40